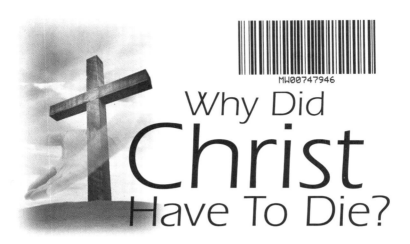

# Why Did Christ Have To Die?

## Discovery Series Bible Study

Couldn't He have accomplished more by living a full and happy life? Think of the people He could have healed, the teaching He could have done, the problems He could have solved. Why was He obsessed with dying? Why didn't He defend Himself in court for the sake of His family, His disciples, and all who admired Him? This booklet, compiled by our staff of writers, takes a look at the reasons given in the Bible why Christ planned and allowed His own death.

Martin R. De Haan II, President of RBC Ministries

Publisher:                             Discovery House Publishers
Editor:                                   David Sper
Graphic Design:             Alex Soh, Janet Chim, Ineke, Felix Xu
Series Coordinator/Study Guide:   Bill Crowder, Sim Kay Tee

This *Discovery Series Bible Study* is based on the *Discovery Series* booklet "Why Did Christ Have To Die?" (Q0202) from RBC Ministries. The *Discovery Series* has more than 140 titles on a variety of biblical and Christian-living issues. These 32-page booklets offer a rich resource of insight for your study of God's Word.
For a catalog of *Discovery Series* booklets, write to RBC Ministries, PO Box 2222, Grand Rapids, MI 49501-2222 or visit us on the Web at: www.discoveryseries.org

# Discovery House Publishers

A member of the RBC Ministries family:
*Our Daily Bread, Day Of Discovery, RBC Radio, Discovery Series, Campus Journal, Discovery House Music, Sports Spectrum*

ISBN 1-57293-086-1

# Table Of Contents

Foreword: Why Did Christ Have To Die?...........1

**Study No. 1—The Controversies Of The Cross (Part 1)**

The Symbol Of The Cross...........4

The Opinions Of The Cross...........5

Study Guide...........6

**Study No. 2—The Controversies Of The Cross (Part 2)**

The Offensiveness Of The Cross...........8

The Dilemma Of The Cross...........9

Study Guide...........12

**Study No. 3—The Impact Of The Cross (Part 1)**

The Resolution Of The Cross...........14

The Principles Of The Cross...........15

Study Guide...........20

**Study No. 4—The Impact Of The Cross (Part 2)**

The Results Of The Cross...........22

The Irony Of The Cross...........24

Study Guide...........28

**Study No. 5—The Elements Of The Cross**

The Background Of The Cross...........30

The Words Of The Cross...........32

The Indictment Of The Cross...........33

The Call Of The Cross...........35

Study Guide...........36

The Satisfaction Of The Cross...........38

Leader's And User's Guide...........40

*Our Daily Bread* Ordering Information...........43

*Discovery Series Bible Study* Ordering Information...........44

# The Symbol Of The Cross

Can you imagine what public reaction would be if a fundamentalist religious group adopted an electric chair as its symbol? Think of what it would be like to see an image of an electric chair on top of their meeting places or as jewelry hanging around their necks.

Yet that's what the cross amounts to. The cross was a means of capital punishment. Crucifixion was the way the Romans put their worst criminals to death. It was horrible—far worse than a gas chamber, firing squad, or even a hangman's noose.

Why, then, do Christians make so much of this instrument of public ridicule and torture? Why are Christians obsessed with this symbol of death? Do they realize what they are doing?

> **The cross has become so widely used as religious jewelry that it has lost much of its original meaning and horror.**

In many cases, the answer seems to be no. Even Christians fail to realize the implications of the cross. It has become so widely used as religious jewelry, as a symbol of love and hope, and even as a sign of good luck that it has lost much of its original meaning and horror. It has become so generally accepted, in fact, that everyone from devoted followers of Christ to atheists wear its image around their necks.

# The Opinions Of The Cross

So what do people think of the cross? More specifically, what do they think of the cross as it relates to Christ? That's where the symbol comes from, and that's where the real discussion begins. Why did a beautiful life have to come to such a terrible end? What was in His mind? What should now be in ours? Here are some of the explanations people give for the death of Christ.

### "It's an example of nonresistance."

Some people feel that when Jesus died on the cross He was giving us the ultimate example of how to live in a violent, hostile world. They say that His death shows us how to live successfully by being strong enough to let others have their way.

### "It means whatever you want it to mean."

Those who take this approach generally believe that Christ did not actually accomplish anything when He died on the cross. Since it has become such a part of our awareness, it can be used to symbolize many different things.

### "It has no real meaning."

Some people say that the significance of Christ was in His life—not in His death. They believe that He came to live a flawless life on earth so that we could know what God is like. But that was all God sent Him to do. His death, they say, was not related to His mission on earth.

### "It represents failure."

Those who hold this view say that Jesus had a noble and global plan for earth, but that He died before He could carry it out. His mission was aborted when the Roman soldiers nailed Him to the cross like a common criminal. When Christ died, these people say, it meant that He had failed.

STUDY
NO. *1*

# The Symbol & Opinions Of The Cross

1 Corinthians 1:18—"The message of the cross is foolishness to those who are perishing, but to us who are being saved it is the power of God."

## Warming Up
How do you think people would respond to a religion that used an electric chair or gas chamber as a symbol of its faith?

## Thinking Through
How much do you know about the actual process of crucifixion? When you think of the horrors of death on a cross, how do you feel?

Consider the statement on page 4, "[The cross] has become so widely used as religious jewelry, as a symbol of love and hope, and even as a sign of good luck that it has lost much of its original meaning and horror." Is this good or bad? Why?

In the different opinions of the cross expressed on page 5, which one do you think is the most dangerous? The most subtle? The most absurd? Why?

## Digging In
### Key Text: Matthew 27:35-44,51-56
As we consider different opinions on the meaning of the cross, it is helpful to see that there were differing views on Christ's crucifixion even as it was happening. In Matthew 27, what six groups/individuals are seen at the cross of Jesus, and what were their different reactions to it?

The religious leaders (vv.41-43) and the women from Galilee (vv.55-56) had very different opinions of the events on the cross. How do you think the religious leaders viewed Jesus' crucifixion? How do you think the women viewed it? Explain your answers. Why were they both wrong?

The centurion was watching the same events on Calvary that day as everyone else. Why do you think his opinion (Mt. 27:54) was so different than the opinion of most of the other spectators there?

## Going Further
### Refer
Compare the four Gospel accounts of the crucifixion. In what ways are they similar? In what ways are they different? (see Mt. 27:33-56; Mk. 15:22-41; Lk.23:26-49; Jn. 19:16-30).

### Reflect
How can we reflect the cross of Christ in our own lives? (see 1 Pet. 2:19-24). What effect can our lives have on how people view the credibility of the gospel? Does your life attract people to the Christ of the cross?

³⁵Then they crucified Him . . . . ³⁷And they put up over His head the accusation written against Him: THIS IS JESUS THE KING OF THE JEWS. ³⁸Then two robbers were crucified with Him, one on the right and another on the left. ³⁹And those who passed by blasphemed Him, wagging their heads ⁴⁰and saying, 'You who destroy the temple and build it in three days, save Yourself! If You are the Son of God, come down from the cross.' ⁴¹Likewise the chief priests also, mocking with the scribes and elders, said, ⁴²'He saved others; Himself He cannot save. If He is the King of Israel, let Him now come down from the cross, and we will believe Him. ⁴³He trusted in God; let Him deliver Him now if He will have Him; for He said, "I am the Son of God."' ⁴⁴Even the robbers who were crucified with Him reviled Him with the same thing. . . . ⁵⁴So when the centurion and those with him, who were guarding Jesus, saw the earthquake and the things that had happened, they feared greatly, saying, 'Truly this was the Son of God!' ⁵⁵And many women who followed Jesus from Galilee, ministering to Him, were there looking on from afar."
*Matthew 27:35-44,54-55*

# The Offensiveness Of The Cross

Some people see so much good in the cross that they fail to see it as a terrible instrument of death. But to others, the cross is so offensive that they fail to see its value.

The apostle Paul said it would be that way. Writing to the Christians at Corinth, he said, "We preach Christ crucified, to the Jews a stumbling block and to the Greeks foolishness" (1 Cor. 1:23).

The apostles' claim that Jesus was the long-awaited Messiah was almost impossible for a Jew to accept. To believe that the Messiah died on the cross was unimaginable—especially since the Old Testament said that anyone who died on a tree was cursed by God (Dt. 21:23). The cross offended them deeply.

The Gentiles too were offended by the cross. In their opinion, it was foolishness. They felt that their logical thinking and good living would satisfy the gods. They saw no reason to believe in the senseless death of an obscure Galilean.

And what about people today? Does the cross still offend? Do people still stumble over its message?

- If their philosophical point of view does not include the reality of sin and the need of a Savior, the answer is yes!
- If by their godly living and high morals they expect to win God's approval, yes!
- If they expect His favor because of their national heritage or family name, yes!
- If they think God is too loving to punish people for their wrongs, yes!

The message of the cross, a first-century "electric chair," will offend them. What we need to realize, however, is that the cross is not just something hard to live with. It actually makes life possible. In fact, the cross resolved the greatest dilemma of all time.

# The Dilemma Of The Cross

The cross resolves two great dilemmas—one from God's perspective and one from man's. All parents can understand the dilemma of not wanting to correct a disobedient child with painful discipline, while at the same time realizing that you can't just blink or yawn at his bad behavior.

What do you do? You love that little one. But he has also clearly disobeyed you, and right now he is lying to you in an attempt to cover it up. Sure, you love him. But you also know that you can't just brush off the problem. He has to be punished—and you've got to do it.

The situation caused by our sin was infinitely more complex than that. But there are some parallels. Because God is a holy God, He cannot just ignore our sin. Yet because He is a loving God, He is not merely willing to let us get what we deserve.

**Because God is holy, He can't just ignore our sin. Yet because He is loving, He is not merely willing to let us get what we deserve.**

Another illustration might help us to see the dilemma from man's perspective. Imagine a group of people trapped on the roof of a high-rise building engulfed in flames. The only way to safety is to jump to the roof of an adjoining building. But it is 30 feet away! In desperation, people begin to attempt the impossible leap. Some jump farther out than others, but all fall to their death.

So it is with man's helpless condition before God. Our sin caused a separation between us and a holy God that cannot be bridged by anything we do. We are utterly helpless to save ourselves. But the love of God provided a way: the cross of Christ.

We might diagram the dilemma like this:

| Holy | GOD | Loving |
|------|-----|--------|
|      |     |        |
| Sinful | MAN | Helpless |

The necessity for Calvary's tree can be traced back to a much earlier tree. All our problems began when our first parents willfully and disobediently ate of the tree of the knowledge of good and evil. God had said that Adam and his wife would die if they ate the fruit of that tree. And they did. From that time on, no man was the man he was created to be. From that time on, the children of Adam were born physically alive but spiritually dead. Not only was the garden paradise lost, but so was the innocence man was created with.

Every child born from Eden until today has proven that innocence was lost. Once created to walk with God, man has inherited a nature that causes him to forget God, to hate his fellowmen, and to live a life of self-destruction. Because of this, David the king of Israel went on record as saying, "Behold, I was brought forth in iniquity, and in sin my mother conceived me" (Ps. 51:5).

And the apostle Paul wrote, "Through one man sin entered the world, and death through sin" (Rom. 5:12) and "the wages of sin is death" (6:23). In another letter he wrote that "in Adam all die" (1 Cor. 15:22).

This is our condition. When Adam followed the way of the serpent, he didn't just hurt himself. When he ate of that tree in defiance of his Maker, spiritual and physical death fell upon all men. And so it has come now to us. The proof is, all of us sinned against God the first chance we got.

Furthermore, we can't do anything to help ourselves. No amount of self-improvement or good deeds can win back what Adam lost. The prophet Isaiah saw this clearly, for he said that our best efforts are nothing better than dirty rags (Isa. 64:6). Much later, the apostle Paul expressed the same awareness (Eph. 2:8-9). His words remind us that no one can pull himself up to God by yanking on his own bootstraps.

This is bad news. But the Bible, the most reliable book in the world, claims to be true. We are born into this world spiritually dead. We are born separated from God. We are born into a world of physical and spiritual death, and unless something happens, we will live out our lives in rebellion against God. Unless something happens, we are destined for the judgment of God—the second death, the lake of fire created for the devil and all of his demons.

**Our sin caused a separation between us and a holy God that cannot be bridged by anything we do. We are utterly helpless to save ourselves.**

And if that were not enough, the Bible tells us that there's not a thing in the world we can do on our own to merit a rescue. Without a doubt, we need help. We need rescue. We need to be delivered from our guilt and bondage—before it is everlastingly too late.

STUDY NO. *2*

# The Offensiveness & Dilemma Of The Cross

Romans 6:23—"The wages of sin is death; but the gift of God is eternal life in Christ Jesus our Lord."

Objective:
**To understand why the cross is a "rock of offense" to many, yet the only solution to our spiritual dilemma.**

Bible Memorization:
**Romans 6:23**

Reading:
**"The Offensiveness & Dilemma Of The Cross" pp.8-11**

## Warming Up
When was the last time you shared the message of the cross with an unbeliever? How would you describe the response?

## Thinking Through
Several reasons are listed on page 8 to explain why some people view the cross as offensive. What are they? Can you think of any others?

What two dilemmas did the death of Christ resolve? (p.9). How did the cross resolve them?

What do you think about the statement in Isaiah 64:6 that our best efforts are nothing better than dirty rags? How do we know Isaiah's words are true? What have you seen in life that supports that idea?

## Digging In
### Key Text: 1 Corinthians 1:18-25
What are the two views of the message of the cross found in verse 18? How did Paul describe the people who hold to each one of these views?

In verses 22-23, Paul said that the Jews and Gentiles desire specific things—but in the message of the cross, each group receives something different from that which they seek. What are they seeking, what are they receiving, and why?

What is Paul's key to resolving the conflict between God's plan and men's desires? (vv.24-25).

## Going Further
### Refer
Compare Paul's discussion of the unfortunate responses of Jews and Gentiles to the message of the cross (1 Cor. 1:18-25) to his own declaration of the power and priority of that message (Rom. 1:16-17). How do the groups mentioned and their reactions differ in these two passages?

### Reflect
Paul wrote, "I am not ashamed of the gospel of Christ, for it is the power of God to salvation for everyone who believes, for the Jew first and also for the Greek" (Rom. 1:16). Do you ever find yourself embarrassed by the gospel message? Why? Do you get frustrated by people's response to it? What can you do about this embarrassment and frustration?

"$^{18}$The message of the cross is foolishness to those who are perishing, but to us who are being saved it is the power of God. $^{19}$For it is written: 'I will destroy the wisdom of the wise, and bring to nothing the understanding of the prudent.' $^{20}$Where is the wise? Where is the scribe? Where is the disputer of this age? Has not God made foolish the wisdom of this world? $^{21}$For since, in the wisdom of God, the world through wisdom did not know God, it pleased God through the foolishness of the message preached to save those who believe. $^{22}$For Jews request a sign, and Greeks seek after wisdom; $^{23}$but we preach Christ crucified, to the Jews a stumbling block and to the Greeks foolishness, $^{24}$but to those who are called, both Jews and Greeks, Christ the power of God and the wisdom of God. $^{25}$Because the foolishness of God is wiser than men, and the weakness of God is stronger than men."
*1 Corinthians 1:18-25*

# The Resolution Of The Cross

When Adam and Eve sinned, God could have struck them dead instantly. And He would have been just in doing so, because His holy nature demands that disobedience be punished by death.

Yet, because God is love, He did not strike our first parents dead. Instead, He sought them out, provided them with a covering of animal skins, and gave to them a wonderful promise (Gen. 3:15). At that point God announced the good news. Yes, the good news is that God Himself resolved the dilemma—His holiness is counter-balanced by His love! Love found a way. Love found another tree, the cross (Rom. 5:6). God in His wisdom provided a way to undo the terrible damage done to man at that first tree.

The tree in the Garden of Eden has now given way to the cross. And on that tree of humiliation, goodness triumphed over evil. Mercy triumphed over justice. The rescue was completed. The mission was accomplished. The dilemma was resolved.

| Holy | GOD | Loving |
|------|-----|--------|
|  | CHRIST |  |
| Sinful | MAN | Helpless |

# The Principles Of The Cross

How did God do it? What did He see in that ugly tree of execution? What happened as His only begotten and dearly loved Son bled, struggled, cried, "It is finished," and then gave up His spirit?

Let's look at two principles of resolution that ended the dilemma caused by our sin and helplessness and God's holiness and love:
1) the principle of adequate sacrifice, and
2) the principle of necessary substitution.

## Principle 1: **The cross provided an adequate sacrifice.**

| Holy | GOD | Loving |
|---|---|---|
| Sacrifice | CHRIST | Sacrifice |
| Sinful | MAN | Helpless |

There can be no forgiveness without a sacrificial death (Heb. 9:22). Through His death on the cross, Jesus Christ presented to God a sacrifice sufficient to pay for the sins of all mankind. The animal deaths of Old Testament days fell far short of that, for they did not actually take away sin.

The Old Testament sacrifices had to be offered every day. Animal after animal was brought to the altar and slain. Each new day brought a new round of sacrificial slayings. The writer of Hebrews, commenting on this fact, said, "For it is not possible that the blood of bulls and goats could take away sins" (Heb. 10:4).

Furthermore, those sacrifices were only for sins committed involuntarily, in ignorance, or through human weakness (Lev. 4:2-7). A sacrifice could not be given for a premeditated, deliberate sin in Old Testament days. That is why David, when he repented of his double sin of adultery with Bathsheba and the murder of Uriah, did not even present a sacrifice. Rather, he came before God with "a broken and contrite heart" to find forgiveness (Ps. 51:16-17).

> **"Now, once at the end of the ages,**
> **He has appeared to put away sin**
> **by the sacrifice of Himself."**
> **—Hebrews 9:26**

By His death on the cross, the Lord Jesus provided a once-for-all sacrifice for all our sins (Heb. 10:12). He was the complete and perfect sacrifice. It satisfied every demand of a holy God, and it brings salvation to all who trust in Christ.

# His sacrifice was adequate for several reasons:

- *He became a member of the human family.* He could truly represent us (something no angel could do) because He took to Himself a human nature.
- *He lived a sinless life.* Confronted by physical, mental, and spiritual temptation, Jesus did not sin (Heb. 4:15). Therefore, when He died, He did so as a perfect human being. Because He did not sin, He could die for our sins.
- *He remained God.* Even though Christ became fully human, He also retained His full deity. He was not half God and half man; He was fully God and fully man. His goodness is what gave His sacrifice infinite value, making it adequate to pay for the sins of all mankind.

# Principle 2: The cross provided a necessary substitute.

| Holy | God | Loving |
|------|-----|--------|
| Substitute | CHRIST | Substitute |
| Sinful | MAN | Helpless |

Jesus had substitution in mind when He told His followers that He would give His life as a "ransom for many" (Mk. 10:45).

Whether they recognized it or not when He said it, His disciples would soon learn that Christ was planning to give His life in exchange for their legal release from sin and guilt. On the cross, Christ would die in their place—and in our place. At Calvary, He died the death all of us should have died, taking the punishment we deserved. "For God so loved the world that He gave His only begotten Son" (Jn. 3:16). Because of our helplessness, God in love sent His Son to be our substitute. He exchanged His life for ours, dying that we might live (Isa. 53:5-6; Rom. 5:8; 1 Cor. 15:3; 2 Cor. 5:21; 1 Pet. 2:24; 3:18).

When Jesus said that He had come to give His life a ransom for many, His hearers probably realized that He had in mind the Jewish sacrificial system. From early childhood they had seen sheep or oxen or turtle doves brought to the altar and killed. They knew that the animal's death was associated with their sins. As they watched the priest place his hand on the forehead of the animal, they realized that this was a symbol of the transfer of guilt from the sinner to the animal. Then, when they saw the beast killed and the blood sprinkled around the altar, they understood that this blood in some way symbolized the taking away of their guilt.

**Because of our helplessness,
God in love sent His Son to be our substitute.
He exchanged His life for ours,
dying that we might live.**

The same principle of the substitute was later fulfilled in the One of whom John the Baptist said, "Behold! The Lamb of God who takes away the sin of the world!" (Jn. 1:29).

This principle is illustrated by a story from American history. In a tribe of Indians, someone was stealing chickens. The chief declared that, if caught, the offender would receive 10 lashes. When the stealing continued, he raised it to 20 lashes. Still the chickens methodically disappeared. In anger, the chief raised the sentence to 100 lashes—a sure sentence of death.

The thief was finally caught. But the chief faced a terrible dilemma. The thief was his own mother!

When the day of penalty came, the whole tribe gathered. Would the chief's love override his justice? The crowd gasped when he ordered his mother to be tied to the whipping post. The chief removed his shirt, revealing his powerful stature, and took the whip in hand. But instead of raising it to strike the first blow, he handed it to a strong, young brave at his side.

Slowly the chief walked over to his mother and wrapped his massive arms around her in an engulfing embrace. Then he ordered the brave to give him the 100 lashes.

That's what Jesus did for us. In love He became our substitute and died in our place. He overcame our inability to save ourselves by paying the price for our sins. In our illustration, a mother's life was extended by the substitutionary love of her son; for us, everlasting life was bought through the substitutionary death of Christ.

> **In love, Jesus became our substitute
> and died in our place. He overcame
> our inability to save ourselves
> by paying the price for our sins.**

The death of Christ, therefore, was of tremendous value, for it bridged the gulf between God and man. Look again at what happened.

## Man's Condition:

Condemned by Adam's sin and his own, and powerless to do anything to save himself, man was under the penalty of death.

## God's Position:

God was bound by His own holiness to punish evil. To do less would be to violate His own character. But because He is also love, He desired to save man from his sentence of death.

## The Resolution:

Christ, God's Son, became human, lived a sinless life, then died on our behalf. His sacrificial, substitutionary death made possible our salvation.

Look at the complete diagram. It shows you how the death of Christ resolved the dilemma.

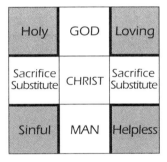

STUDY
NO. **3**

# The Resolution & Principles Of The Cross

Mark 10:45—"Even the Son of Man did not come to be served, but to serve, and to give His life a ransom for many."

Objective:

**To understand what Christ accomplished on our behalf on the cross, and why it was an adequate sacrifice.**

Bible Memorization:
**Mark 10:45**

Reading:
**"The Resolution & Principles Of The Cross" pp.14-19**

## Warming Up

Has anyone ever made a significant sacrifice for you? If so, how did it make you feel? How did it change the way you viewed that person?

## Thinking Through

What two trees are at the heart of Christianity? (p.14). How are they connected? How does God use the second tree to overcome the damage done by the first tree?

On page 16 we are given several reasons why the sacrifice of Christ was adequate. What are those reasons, and how does each of them become a source of hope for us?

Christ died in our place as our substitute (see pp.17-18). How does His role as "substitute" bridge the gulf between God and man, and what benefits do we receive as a result?

## Digging In
### Key Text: Hebrews 9:22

What is the context of this verse? How does this discussion of Passover prepare for the following discussion of Christ's sacrifice?

Why is the shedding of blood so significant in the redemptive plan of God? (see Lev. 17:11).

## Going Further
### Refer

Compare the statement of Hebrews 9:22 about the necessity of a blood sacrifice to the following passages: Genesis 3:1-21, Exodus 12, 1 John 1:5-10. How do these passages support Hebrews 9:22? How are they distinct from Hebrews 9:22?

"According to the law almost all things are purified with blood, and without shedding of blood there is no remission."
### Hebrews 9:22

### Reflect

Our forgiveness was costly to Jesus. He paid for it with His own blood. Reflect on the words of several hymns (*And Can It Be, Nothing But The Blood, There Is A Fountain*) that express worship for Christ's sacrifice for our sins. Then respond to Him with your own heart of worship and praise.

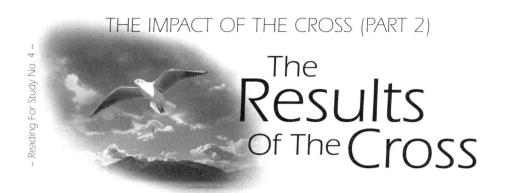

# The Results Of The Cross

The death of Jesus Christ 2,000 years ago was not just a heroic act that caught the imagination of a band of religious idealists. Nor was it an act of weakness.

It was a loving, courageous, death-defying mission of rescue. The result is that the person who trusts in Jesus Christ is changed in his relationship to God. He is changed in his relationship to his own sin. And his future is changed, both for this life and the life to come.

> **If we could merit our own salvation,**
> **Christ would never have died**
> **to provide it.**

That change is spelled out in four basic concepts that show the results of what Christ did for us. Here is what is ours once we have accepted the sacrificial, substitutionary death of Christ.

## 1. Reconciliation: We are at peace with God.

When Jesus Christ died on the cross, He made it possible for us to be reconciled to God and restored to fellowship with Him by faith in Christ. Enmity is turned to friendship, alienation to sonship, hostility to faith, and hatred to love because of Christ's sacrifice on the cross (Rom. 5:1,10; 2 Cor. 5:18-20; Eph. 2:16; Col. 1:20-22).

## 2. Justification: We are declared right before God.

When Jesus Christ died, He absorbed our punishment. Therefore, when we believe in Him, our sins are no longer held against us (Rom. 3:24; 4:5; 5:1,9; 3:30-31; Ti. 3:4-7).

## 3. Redemption: We are ransomed from our sin and condemnation.

The death of Christ also means we have been bought out of bondage to sin and Satan. The ransom price for our sin has been paid in full (Mt. 20:28; Rom. 3:24; Cor. 1:30; Gal. 3:13; 4:4-5; Eph. 1:7; Col. 1:14; Ti. 2:14; Heb. 9:12; 1 Pet. :18-19).

> **When Jesus Christ died, He absorbed our punishment.**
> **Therefore, when we believe in Him, our sins**
> **are no longer held against us.**

## 4. Propitiation: We are free from God's wrath.

This is possible because an acceptable offering has been made on our behalf. The offering has been made to appease God, to turn His wrath from us (Rom. 3:25; Heb. 2:17; 1 Jn 2:2; 4:10).

# THE IMPACT OF THE CROSS (PART 2)

# The Irony Of The Cross

The irony of all this is that something as ugly as the cross—something revolting enough to cause people to reject the best Man who ever lived—is actually our only hope of rescue from our spiritual helplessness. That's what the Bible says. And that's what Christ confirmed when He rose triumphantly from the dead. The cross was not a mistake. It wasn't a good life falling on bad times. The irony of the cross is that (1) it is the greatest example of God's love, and that (2) in dying, Christ also showed us how to live.

## The first point of irony is this:
## Christ's Death Demonstrated God's Love

The great truth of the most familiar and best-loved verse of the Bible is that the cross was evidence of God's love. "For God so loved the world that He gave His only begotten Son, that whoever believes in Him should not perish but have everlasting life" (Jn. 3:16). A parallel passage reads, "By this we know love, because He laid down His life for us" (1 Jn. 3:16).

Some people look for God's love in nature. But they won't find it guaranteed there, because the message of the created world gives conflicting messages. Sometimes it seems to tell us that God is wonderfully loving. The warm sunshine, the gentle rain, the blooming flowers of the fields, and the watchful care of a cow for her calf all seem to say, "God is love."

At other times, however, the message of nature is quite the opposite. Sun and drought make the ground hard and unproductive. A killer tornado may roar out of a darkened sky without warning. A nest of young rabbits may be killed by a nightstalking cat or foraging jackal. Or an erupting volcano may wipe out entire illages, killing hundreds and making thousands homeless. No, the love of God annot always be seen in nature.

Nor is God's love clearly evident in history. A family of immigrants to the Jnited States from Vietnam or Korea may say that coming to the USA proved to hem that God loves them. But if you talk to the young mother of three children vhose husband was just killed by airplane hijackers, she may scoff bitterly at the dea that a loving God controls all events. Many of the Jewish people who lived hrough the horrors of Auschwitz or Dachau would also reject the idea that God's ove is demonstrated in history.

When Christians talk about God's love being made known, therefore, they must point to something else as evidence. According to the Bible, that evidence is the cross. Because Jesus Christ is God's Son, His death was a profound declaration of God's love.

## In the cross
## we see God's love at its best
## and our sin at its worst.

God has shown His love for us—but at great cost. In the person of Jesus Christ, God became a member of the human family. He lived His whole life without sin. Then, though innocent Himself, He died a terrible death to make our salvation possible. Shining through the darkness that surrounded Calvary that fateful day was the wondrous brilliance of the love of God. Think for a moment about what Christ suffered, and remember that it was for us.

*Stand in awe* as He agonizes before God the Father in Gethsemane until His sweat becomes like great drops of blood falling to the ground.

*Follow in horror* as He is arrested like a criminal, mutilated by a Roman whip, and tortured, mocked, and derided with a crown of thorns.

*Weep for Him* as He stumbles under the heavy wooden beam He is forced to carry to His place of execution.

*Cringe in revulsion* as hardened Roman soldiers pound spikes through His hands, drive nails through His feet, and roughly drop the beam into place.

*Listen to Him* as He hangs there on the cross, praying for His enemies, talking lovingly to His mother, and promising salvation to the criminal who repents.

*Be still* as you see the sky grow black at noon, and as you sit through the 3 hours of eerie midday darkness.

*Listen* to His cry of abandonment, "My God, My God, why have You forsaken Me?"

*Remember* that on the cross, Jesus endured the agony of hell for you and me. God was His Father. He had existed with Him from all eternity in a relationship closer than anything we could ever know. Yet the Father "made Him who knew no sin to be sin for us, that we might become the righteousness of God in Him" (2 Cor. 5:21).

## The second point of irony is:
# Christ's Death Showed Us How To Live

Not only did the cross give us the highest evidence of God's love, but it also provided us with a spiritual principle of life. The love that led Jesus Christ to this unparalleled deed of self-sacrifice was an example for us.

We are to love as He loved; to live as He lived. The Lord Jesus had the cross in mind the evening before His crucifixion when He told His disciples, "A new commandment I give to you, that you love one another; as I have loved you, that you also love one another" (Jn. 13:34). Calvary love is to be standard for our love.

Jesus Christ also had His death on the cross in view when He said this: "Unless a grain of wheat falls into the ground and dies, it remains alone; but if it dies, it produces much grain. He who loves his life will lose it, and he who hates his life in this world will keep it for eternal life. If anyone serves Me, let him follow Me" (Jn. 12:24-26).

This is the law of the harvest: A seed must die before it can produce a plant. Jesus Christ was the "seed" that had to die. Yet His death produced spiritual life for all who would trust Him. We are the fruit of His suffering and death.

But the law of death to bring life did not end with Christ's cross. Jesus declared that it also applies to His followers. We must take the way of the cross, the way of dying to our own selfish desires, if we are to bear the kind of fruit that God created us to produce (Eph. 2:8-10).

> **"Christ also suffered for us,**
> **leaving us an example,**
> **that you should follow His steps."**
> **—1 Peter 2:21**

The apostle Paul saw this principle in Christ's death. Time and again he spoke of being crucified with Christ, of dying to self, and of walking the Calvary road. With deep conviction he wrote, "God forbid that I should glory except in the cross of our Lord Jesus Christ, by whom the world has been crucified to me, and I to the world" (Gal. 6:14).

Because the cross of Christ was Paul's inspiration and confidence, he could write off the world-system as something useless and dead. He saw nothing in it to attract him.

When we live by the law of the harvest, we will be fruitful in our service for Christ. Following His example, we must first die to self. As we do, we will be able to say with Paul, "I have been crucified with Christ; it is no longer I who live, but Christ lives in me; and the life which I now live in the flesh I live by faith in the Son of God, who loved me and gave Himself for me" (Gal. 2:20).

Here again is the irony of the cross. Not only does it bring God's life to us, but it brings our life to God.

STUDY
NO. **4**

# The Results & Irony Of The Cross

2 Corinthians 5:21—"He made Him who knew no sin to be sin for us, that we might become the righteousness of God in Him."

Objective:
**To understand how Christ's death demonstrated God's love for us while we were still in our sin.**

Bible Memorization:
**2 Corinthians 5:21**

Reading:
**"The Results & Irony Of The Cross" pp.22-27**

## Warming Up

We admire heroes that sacrifice themselves for others. Who are some of those heroes in history, or some you have known in your own experience?

## Thinking Through

On pages 22-23, we are told of four important results of Christ's death on the cross. What are they and why is each significant to your relationship with God?

The first of the ironies mentioned in this section (p.24) dealt with God's love being revealed by Christ's death. Why is it demonstrated in the cross, yet not seen so clearly in nature and in history?

The second irony spoke of Christ's death showing us how to live. Why does the law of the harvest explain how we receive life through the death of Jesus?

## Digging In
### Key Text: John 12:24-26

In the context of chapter 12, where was Jesus when He made the declaration of the "grain of wheat"? What was the purpose behind this analogy? What prompted the comment to begin with? What are the implications of Jesus' comments in verse 25 about loving your life versus hating your life? How did Christ apply this to Himself in verse 27?

Compare Jesus' words in verse 26 ("where I am, there will My servant also be") to His later words in John 14:1-4. How are they similar? How are they different?

## Going Further

### Refer

Compare Jesus' words in John 12:24-26 to Paul's words in 1 Corinthians 15. How are the same ideas used to express the very different themes of death (Jn. 12) and resurrection? (1 Cor. 15).

### Reflect

On pages 25-26, we are challenged to see the awful depths of the suffering of Christ for our sins and our life, and our appropriate responses to Him. Spend several moments in thoughtful prayer and consideration of each of these responses.

"$^{24}$Most assuredly, I say to you, unless a grain of wheat falls into the ground and dies, it remains alone; but if it dies, it produces much grain. $^{25}$He who loves his life will lose it, and he who hates his life in this world will keep it for eternal life. $^{26}$If anyone serves Me, let him follow Me; and where I am, there My servant will be also. If anyone serves Me, him My Father will honor."
*John 12:24-26*

# The Background Of The Cross

We are fortunate to be able to look back to the cross and see it in perspective. The first disciples of Christ were not so privileged. For them the crucifixion came as a terrible, heart-rending tragedy. Their beloved Leader was dead. Their hopes of a messianic kingdom had evaporated. Their enemies were cheering. They were stunned by the unexpected twist of events. Only later, when Christ surprised them with His resurrected presence, did the disciples begin to understand that the Old Testament pointed to a cross as well as to a kingdom. Only then did they begin to see that Christ had to fulfill the picture of a suffering Servant before He could return as the promised King.

The resurrected Jesus explained to His astonished followers how the cross was part of the plan of God. First, He showed them His wounds. Then He said, "These are the words which I spoke to you while I was still with you, that all things must be fulfilled which were written in the Law of Moses and the Prophets and the Psalms concerning Me" (Lk. 24:44). He opened their minds to the Old Testament pictures and prophecies about His death (v.45). Let's leaf through the Old Testament for examples of each.

## Old Testament Prophecies Of Christ's Death

| | |
|---|---|
| Genesis 3:15 | The Seed of woman "bruised" |
| Psalm 16:10 | Messiah not left in the grave |
| Psalm 22:1 | Messiah's cry of forsakenness |
| Psalm 22:6-8 | Messiah mocked |
| Psalm 22:15 | Messiah's thirst |
| Psalm 22:16 | Messiah's pierced hands and feet |
| Psalm 22:17 | The stares of Messiah's enemies |

| | |
|---|---|
| Psalm 22:18 | Gambling for Messiah's garments |
| Psalm 69:21 | Vinegar offered to Messiah |
| Isaiah 49:7 | God's Servant despised |
| Isaiah 50:6 | Messiah physically abused |
| Isaiah 52:14 | Messiah's face disfigured |
| Isaiah 53:5 | Messiah pierced for our sins |
| Isaiah 53:7 | Messiah silent before His accusers |
| Isaiah 53:9 | Messiah's grave among the rich |
| Isaiah 53:12 | Messiah identified with criminals |
| Daniel 9:26 | God's anointed One "cut off" |
| Zechariah 12:10 | Messiah "pierced" by Israel |
| Zechariah 13:7 | The Shepherd struck down |

# Old Testament Pictures Of Christ's Death

The imagery of the cross appears in three Old Testament pictures.

SACRIFICES. The substitutionary death of Christ is most often pictured in the Old Testament by the sacrificial system. The provision of animal skins for Adam and Eve is seen by many Bible scholars as God's initiative to provide for man's sin by means of sacrifice (Gen. 3:21). The Passover sacrifice is a primary image of deliverance through the shed blood of a lamb (Ex. 12; Lev. 23; 1 Cor. 5:7; 1 Pet. 1:19). John the Baptist connected the animal sacrifice and Jesus Christ when he cried, "Behold! The Lamb of God who takes away the sin of the world!" (Jn. 1:29). An extensive explanation is given in Hebrews 9:11–10:18.

THE BRONZE SERPENT. Israel was afflicted with the bites of serpents because of their disobedience. At God's instruction, a serpent was made out of bronze and placed atop a pole in the center of the camp. All who looked at it were healed of their snakebites (Num. 21:4-9). Christ would be "lifted up" and all who looked on Him in faith would experience spiritual healing (Jn. 3:14-15).

JONAH. Jesus taught that the experience of Jonah in the belly of the great fish for 3 days and 3 nights was a picture of His own death, burial, and resurrection (Mt. 12:39-41).

By prophecies and pictures, therefore, the Old Testament looked forward to the death of Christ. His crucifixion was not an unforeseen detour in the plan of God. Rather, it was the reason that He came.

# The Words Of The Cross

Even in dying, Christ was teaching us how to live. The seven recorded statements from the cross give us seven profound lessons on life.

**1** "Father, forgive them, for they do not know what they do" (Lk. 23:34).
Forgiveness is better than revenge.

**2** "Assuredly, I say to you, today you will be with Me in Paradise" (Lk. 23:43).
Faith is rewarded with promise.

**3** "Woman, behold your Son! . . . Behold your mother!" (Jn. 19:26-27).
Our own needs should not overshadow the needs of others.

**4** "My God, My God, why have You forsaken Me?" (Mk. 15:34).
Anything that could jeopardize our relationship with God should produce anguish.

**5** "I thirst" (Jn. 19:28).
These words, spoken to fulfill prophecy, remind us of the authority of Scripture.

**6** "It is finished" (Jn. 19:30).
Do not let yourself lose sight of your goal of doing God's will.

**7** "Father, into Your hands I commend My spirit" (Lk. 23:46).
In your suffering, entrust yourself to God.

# The Indictment Of The Cross

n the Bible are astonishing words that will testify forever to the wickedness of nan. Describing the execution of Jesus Christ, the gospel writers used the statement, "They crucified Him." Never before had One so innocent endured such an outpouring of human scorn and contempt. The whole process was a terrifying revelation of human sin.

**In the Bible, the astonishing statement, "They crucified Him," will testify forever to the wickedness of man.**

*First,* there was the jealous hatred of the religious leaders of Israel. The Pharisees, Sadducees, and scribes joined forces to discredit Jesus (Mt. 22:15-46). They resented His popularity (Mt. 21:45-46; Jn. 12:19). They said His miracles were works of Satan (Mt. 12:22-30). They were appalled at His acceptance of ordinary people (Lk. 15:1-2). They hated His exposure of their hypocrisy (Mt. 15:1-14). Although they were looked up to as the spiritual leaders of Israel, they falsely accused, illegally tried, condemned, and crucified the One sent from God (Mt. 26–27).

*Second,* there was the greedy betrayal by Judas. As one of the disciples, he shared in the life and ministry of Jesus. The teachings, the miracles, the very heart and soul of the Savior were his to experience. But in the end, Judas chose to betray Him. As treasurer of the Twelve, he often stole from the common purse

(Jn. 12:6). It is therefore no surprise that he would sell his own soul, and the Savior, for 30 pieces of silver (Mt. 26:14-16).

*Third,* there was the cunning cowardice of Pontius Pilate, the governor of Palestine appointed by Caesar. He was hated by the Jewish leaders. He knew they were manipulating him into killing Jesus, and he resisted it. All of his counter moves failed. Although he publicly proclaimed Christ's innocence, he did not set Him free. Giving in to pressure, he ordered the crucifixion of Christ.

*Fourth,* there is the fickle desire of the crowd. A few days earlier, the masses had cried, "Hosanna to the son of David," as Christ entered Jerusalem. But now they clamored for His death, shouting, "Crucify Him! Crucify Him!"

> **"Pilate, . . . wishing to release Jesus,**
> **again called out to them.**
> **But they shouted, saying,**
> **'Crucify Him, crucify Him!' "**
> **—Luke 23:20-21**

*Fifth,* there was the heartless cruelty of the Roman soldiers. They stripped Him and beat Him. They mocked Him. They spit on Him. They twisted a crown of thorns onto His head. They led Him away, bruised and bleeding, and crucified Him. What monstrous behavior!

Now, it would be easy for us to condemn these people. But let's be honest. Those wicked deeds against the innocent Son of God represent the truth about all of us. They are an indictment of our own sin.

# The Call Of The Cross

Look again at the cross. Look at the One dying there. He never sinned, yet He is on the cross to bear the penalty for the sins of the whole world. He's dying there on your behalf. That should be you on that cross.

It's an ugly scene, isn't it? It shows us how terrible sin really is, and what a horrible price had to be paid to set us free from it. If you are a Christian, coming one more time to the cross should fill your heart with gratitude for what Christ did for you there. As your sacrifice and substitute, He made it possible for you to be forgiven and to be saved from your sin. Why don't you give Him your thanks right now? Then determine to walk in obedience to God.

If you are not a Christian, won't you trust Him as your Savior? Your sin is real. You cannot do anything at all about it—except to trust in Jesus Christ. Don't wait. Tell Him that you believe in Him as your personal Savior. Ask Him to save you. He will, because it was for you that He died on that excruciating cross. He was your sacrifice. He paid the penalty for your sin. Trust Him now!

> **"God so loved the world
> that He gave His only begotten Son,
> that whoever believes in Him
> should not perish
> but have everlasting life."
> —John 3:16**

STUDY
NO. **5**

# The Background, Words, Indictment, & Call Of The Cross

John 3:14-15—"As Moses lifted up the serpent in the wilderness, even so must the Son of Man be lifted up, that whoever believes in Him should not perish but have eternal life."

Objective:

**To grasp the details of God's work on the cross and to respond to it.**

Bible Memorization:

**John 3:14-15**

Reading:

**"The Background, Words, Indictment, & Call Of The Cross" pp.30-35**

## Warming Up

Imagine the emotions the disciples felt as a result of the crucifixion of Jesus. What do you think was the dominant emotion—fear or disappointment? Why? Can you imagine what your emotional response might have been?

## Thinking Through

On page 31, we are reminded of several of the Old Testament pictures that were fulfilled in the death of Christ. What were those pictures and how did the crucifixion of Jesus fulfill them?

In the words of Christ from the cross (p.32), which were directed to the Father, and which were directed to the people at the cross? Which dealt with the specific mission of Christ (the forgiveness of sins), and which dealt with other concerns of Christ?

How do the indictments of the cross (listed on pp.33-34) reveal the true nature of human sin? How does the cross address these and all other issues of sin in human beings?

## Digging In
### Key Text: Psalm 22:15-18

In verse 15, the psalmist vividly described one of the physical consequences of crucifixion (dehydration).

Where is this paralleled in the Gospel accounts of the death of Christ? What are the implications of this condition being clearly prophesied hundreds of years before crucifixion was invented?

The description of the crucifixion in verses 16-17 contains several significant elements. Which elements are physical and which are emotional? What is meant by the symbolic reference to "dogs"?

Perhaps the most amazing of these prophecies is the pinpoint accuracy of verse 18. How does this prophetic portrait of the details of Christ's death provide a commentary on the eternal purposes of God to save lost people?

## Going Further
### Refer
The Gospels are filled with expressions of the compassion and concern of Christ for a lost race—and His mission to rescue us. In light of that, what are some passages where Jesus expresses His concern—a concern that was ultimately fulfilled in the cross?

### Reflect
Have you received the forgiveness Christ offers through His death on the cross for you? If not, by faith, will you confess your sin and accept His gift of forgiveness and eternal life? If you are already a child of God, give praise to the Savior for His great salvation!

"¹⁵My strength is dried up like a potsherd, and My tongue clings to My jaws; You have brought Me to the dust of death. ¹⁶For dogs have surrounded Me; the congregation of the wicked has enclosed Me. They pierced My hands and My feet; ¹⁷I can count all My bones. They look and stare at Me. ¹⁸They divide My garments among them, And for My clothing they cast lots."
*Psalm 22:15-18*

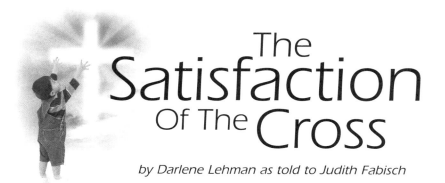

# The Satisfaction
## Of The Cross

*by Darlene Lehman as told to Judith Fabisch*

If there was ever a time I didn't want to be accepted by God, I don't remember it. Our home was religious. Grandmother never had to force me to go to church on Sunday or Holy Days. After school, I often stopped at the cool, dimly lit cathedral near our house and knelt in one of the empty pews. It was a devotion of agony. I wanted God's forgiveness so badly, but He always seemed so very far away.

> **"I wanted God's forgiveness
> so badly, but He always seemed
> so very far away."**

When I was about 10, the bishop visited our cathedral. While he was there, he blessed some holy water. Grandmother sent me to get a bottle of it to put in the small vials scattered around our home. I ran all the way to the cathedral, but I walked home much more slowly. I was thinking hard. I wanted so much to be accepted by God. Impulsively, I drank the holy water! Grandmother could not be angry with me, for she understood the guilt and desire that can be in a young girl's heart. But still I was not satisfied.

High school did not remove the thirst that was in my soul, but I was soon occupied with studies, friends, and dating. Within a year of graduation I met and married Dick. It wasn't long before I was settled into the routine of establishing a home and family.

Although I loved my husband and my home, I longed more than ever for spiritual peace. I increased my acts of devotion to my church, attending faithfully and doing extra things to try to meet God's approval. But I still came away empty. I even went to an evangelistic meeting downtown. But I didn't understand what was being said, so I walked away frustrated. I was ready to do anything to please God.

**"I begged God. I cried out to Him.
I pleaded with Him to reveal Himself to me.
And the answer finally came
from an unexpected place."**

I begged God. I cried out to Him. I pleaded with Him to reveal Himself to me. And the answer finally came from an unexpected place—through my mother-in-law. A sense of peace surrounded her, and she was always very kind. So when she asked me to attend a Christian women's club meeting with her, I was glad to go. A missionary was speaking. In clear, loving, unmistakable terms, she brought us to the cross. I understood for the first time the meaning of Christ's death—praise God! I realized that I should have come here—to the cross—a long time ago. I knew that the thirst of my soul would be satisfied here. I accepted the love and forgiveness of God. With tears of joy, I trusted Christ and His sacrifice for me.

The years have not been easy since. In time I left my church because of the emptiness of its ritual. I grew rapidly in Christ and in my commitment to Him. Dick didn't understand, and eventually he left me. But the Lord has sustained me and the children throughout the years.

The peace and satisfaction I found at the cross has been real—far greater than could ever be found in a bottle of holy water. The forgiveness of sins and acceptance by a holy God can be found only at the cross.

# Discovery Series Bible Study Leader's And User's Guide

## Statement Of Purpose

The *Discovery Series Bible Study* (DSBS) series provides assistance to pastors and leaders in discipling and teaching Christians through the use of RBC Ministries *Discovery Series* booklets. The DSBS series uses the inductive Bible-study method to help Christians understand the Bible more clearly.

## Study Helps

Listed at the beginning of each study are the key verse, objective, and memorization verses. These will act as the compass and map for each study.

Some key Bible passages are printed out fully. This will help the students to focus on these passages and to examine and compare the Bible texts more easily—leading to a better understanding of their meanings. Serious students are encouraged to open their own Bible to examine the other Scriptures as well.

## How To Use DSBS (for individuals and small groups)

### Individuals—Personal Study
- Read the designated pages of the book.
- Carefully consider and answer all the questions.

### Small Groups—Bible-Study Discussion
- To maximize the value of the time spent together, each member should do the lesson work prior to the group meeting.
- Recommended discussion time: 45–55 minutes.
- Engage the group in a discussion of the questions, seeking full participation from each of the members.

# Overview Of Lessons

| Study | Topic | Bible Text | Reading | Questions |
|---|---|---|---|---|
| 1 | The Symbol Of The Cross | Mt. 27:35-56 | pp.4-5 | pp.6-7 |
|   | The Opinions Of The Cross | | | |
| 2 | The Offensiveness Of The Cross | 1 Cor. 1:18-25 | pp.8-11 | pp.12-13 |
|   | The Dilemma Of The Cross | | | |
| 3 | The Resolution Of The Cross | Heb. 9:22 | pp.14-19 | pp.20-21 |
|   | The Principles Of The Cross | | | |
| 4 | The Results Of The Cross | Jn. 12:24-26 | pp.22-27 | pp.28-29 |
|   | The Irony Of The Cross | | | |
| 5 | The Background Of The Cross | Ps. 22:15-18 | pp.30-35 | pp.36-37 |
|   | The Words Of The Cross | | | |
|   | The Indictment Of The Cross | | | |
|   | The Call Of The Cross | | | |

The DSBS format incorporates a "layered" approach to Bible study that includes four segments. These segments form a series of perspectives that become increasingly more personalized and focused. These segments are:

**Warming Up.** In this section, a general interest question is used to begin the discussion (in small groups) or "to get the juices flowing" (in personal study). It is intended to begin the process of interaction at the broadest, most general level.

**Thinking Through.** Here, the student or group is invited to interact with the *Discovery Series* material that has been read. In considering the information and implications of the booklet, these questions help to drive home the critical concepts of that portion of the booklet.

**Digging In.** Moving away from the *Discovery Series* material, this section isolates a key biblical text from the manuscript and engages the student or group in a brief inductive study of that passage of Scripture. This brings the authority of the Bible into the forefront of the study as we consider its message to our hearts and lives.

**Going Further.** This final segment contains two parts. In *Refer*, the student or group has the opportunity to test the ideas of the lesson against the rest of the Bible by cross-referencing the text with other verses. In *Reflect*, the student or group is challenged to personally apply the lesson by making a practical response to what has been learned.

# Pulpit Sermon Series (for pastors and church leaders)

Although the *Discovery Series Bible Study* is primarily for personal and group study, pastors may want to use this material as the foundation for a series of messages on this important issue. The suggested topics and their corresponding texts are as follows:

| Sermon No. | Topic | Text |
|---|---|---|
| 1 | The Controversies Of The Cross (Pt. 1) | Mt. 27:35-56 |
| 2 | The Controversies Of The Cross (Pt. 2) | 1 Cor. 1:18-25 |
| 3 | The Impact Of The Cross (Pt. 1) | Heb. 9:22 |
| 4 | The Impact Of The Cross (Pt. 2) | Jn. 12:24-26 |
| 5 | The Elements Of The Cross | Ps. 22:15-18 |

# Final Thoughts

The DSBS will provide an opportunity for growth and ministry. To internalize the spiritual truths of each study in a variety of environments, the material is arranged to allow for flexibility in the application of the truths discussed.

Whether DSBS is used in small-group Bible studies, adult Sunday school classes, adult Bible fellowships, men's and women's study groups, or church-wide applications, the key to the strength of the discussion will be found in the preparation of each participant. Likewise, the effectiveness of personal and pastoral use of this material will be directly related to the time committed to using this resource.

As you use, teach, or study this material, may you "grow in the grace and knowledge of our Lord and Savior Jesus Christ" (2 Pet. 3:18).

# OUR DAILY BREAD

## Delivered right to your home!

What could be better than getting *Our Daily Bread?* How about having it delivered directly to your home?

You'll also have the opportunity to receive special offers or Bible-study booklets. And you'll get articles written on timely topics we all face, such as forgiveness and anger.

To order your copy of *Our Daily Bread,* write to us at:

**USA: PO Box 2222, Grand Rapids, MI 49501-2222**
**CANADA: Box 1622, Windsor, ON N9A 6Z7**
RBC Web site: www.odb.org/guide

*Support for RBC Ministries comes from the gifts of our members and friends. We are not funded or endowed by any group or denomination.*

◆**Joseph: Overcoming Life's Challenges**
48-page/5-week study on God's faithfulness.
Item # FSU-ZY507

◆**The Lord Is My Shepherd**
48-page/6-week study on Psalm 23.
Item # FSU-Z3673

◆**Jesus' Blueprint For Prayer**
40-page/5-week study on The Lord's Prayer.
Item # FSU-H3431

◆**What Can We Know About The Endtimes?**
48-page/6-week study on endtimes prophecy.
Item # FSU-MW443

◆**Why Would A Good God Allow Suffering?**
48-page/6-week study on the problem of suffering.
Item # FSU-SK375

◆**Does God Want Me Well?**
46-page/4-week study on sickness and healing.
Item # FSU-CE513

◆**Why Did Christ Have To Die?**
44-page/5-week study on Christ's crucifixion.
Item # FSU-LZ401

◆**Did Christ Really Rise From The Dead?**
48-page/6-week study on Christ's resurrection.
Item # FSU-XN702

◆**What If It's True?**
44-page/4-week study on the basics of faith.
Item # FSU-L1471

◆**How Can A Parent Find Peace Of Mind?**
50-page/5-week study on parenting.
Item # FSU-F0758

## Minimum order of 10 guides in any combination
### $2.95 each ($4.45 CAN) Plus shipping & handling

Order online at:
# www.dhp.org/biblestudyguide/
## Credit Card orders call: 1-800-653-8333

Discovery House Publishers    Box 3566
Grand Rapids MI 49501
a member of the RBC Ministries family    fax: 616-957-5741